HOW TO DRAW

FARM ANIMALS

BY ARTHUR ZAIDENBERG

ABELARD-SCHUMAN
LONDON   NEW YORK   TORONTO

BOOKS BY ARTHUR ZAIDENBERG
How to Draw Wild Animals
How to Draw Dogs, Cats and Horses
How to Draw Farm Animals
How to Draw Ships and Trains, Cars and Airplanes
How to Draw Birds, Fish and Reptiles
How to Draw Historic and Modern Bridges
How to Draw Landscapes, Seascapes and Cityscapes
How to Draw Butterflies, Bees and Beetles
How to Draw Flowers, Fruit and Vegetables
How to Draw Costumes and Clothes
How to Draw Military and Civilian Uniforms
How to Draw Athletes in Action
How to Draw Period Costumes
How to Draw Heads and Faces

CONTENTS

BASIC DRAWING MATERIALS

PENCILS

You are at home with the pencil. From your kindergarten days it has been your daily companion and has almost become a part of your hand — like another finger that writes and draws.

Why struggle with a strange tool if you know and understand the pencil so well? Get several pencils of different lead thicknesses so that you may make lines that are heavy and black or thin and light, as you wish. Keep them sharp with your pencil sharpener. There is no special way to hold a pencil for drawing. Any position that you are used to and find comfortable is the right one for *you* to use.

ERASERS

It is best to avoid erasing, as much as possible. If you keep your first *sketch* lines very light you can make the ones you decide to keep darker, and the ones you want to lose will then almost disappear. If you must erase get two different kinds of erasers: a *soap eraser*, which is the soft, crumbly kind, and a *kneaded eraser*, which is very good for erasing pencil lines without smudging. But, I repeat, don't rely on your eraser too much. Draw your lines as if you didn't own an eraser, and soon you'll find you don't really need one.

PAPERS

Almost any paper upon which pencil lines show is good "drawing paper." Ordinary white typewriter paper or your own notebooks (unlined) will be good enough for most drawings. What is important is that it be a pleasant surface and that you have a wad of the same paper or a heavy sheet of blotting paper underneath so that the surface is not too hard for easy drawing.

CRAYONS

If you like to work with crayons, make your first outlines in pencil or with a very sharp pointed crayon so that your drawing is not too rough and fuzzy as many crayon drawings are.

PEN AND INK

Only if you are used to working neatly with a pen should you use it for sketching. However, if you can control a pen and feel at home with it, it is a beautiful tool for drawing. Art supply stores now sell india ink fountain pens quite cheaply and they are very good.

SKETCH PAD

Get a good thick sketch pad small enough to fit in your pocket. Take it everywhere with you and draw every animal you see or, for that matter, anything else you see that appeals to you. Drawing must become a habit if you want to do it very well. A filled sketch book is a fine record of your experiences and a great way to develop your skill.

FOREWORD: FARM ANIMALS

Animals that live among humans take on some of the traits of humans. But "domestic" animals were not always "domesticated," not always at home with us.

Prehistoric man roamed the earth as a hunter. The cattle and other animals he hunted were quite different from those of today. We know this from drawings and paintings of them which were made hundreds of thousands of years ago. They were fierce and wild, far more like the jungle and plain beasts we still hunt than like the calm, dignified farm companions of today.

Our cows, sheep, goats, pigs, horses and other barnyard creatures live with us in our most tranquil places and meet us in our most peaceful moods. They are valuable to us and are treated gently and well. In turn, they have learned to be gentle and to feel secure.

The alert fearfulness which is characteristic of jungle animals is gone from the domestic ones.

The difference is a major one and should be brought out in your drawings. A flock of sheep or a herd of goats or cows is a restful sight, and the realization of this quiet calm must appear in your portrayals.

It is not easy for most children nowadays to become acquainted with farm animals. They are maintained on farms, fenced off from the roads and remote from the cities. Except for the relatively small number of farm-born youngsters, the animals which are so indispensable to our existence are unfamiliar to us.

Of course, you have seen photographs and paintings of

farm animals. But "seeing" is not necessarily "knowing," and for drawing purposes "knowing" or "personal acquaintance" is a valuable thing.

Try to get to the country with your sketch book. Observe the nature and character of each farm animal as well as its appearance and movements.

Action is as important as shape and proportion. Note the manner in which each animal moves, how it stretches its legs, how it stands to eat.

Nothing is hard to draw if you remember that you should not attempt to make an exact copy of what you see, but rather to give your impression of it. This means that you are telling those who see your drawing how you feel about the thing you draw. Your drawing can be very simple, even just a few lines, but if you really try to tell the story, it will be more like the object you draw than if you put in every tiny detail.

In these pages you will meet the animals in their simplest forms. Study their natures, proportions and movements and read the descriptions.

Practice these techniques in drawing the animals, then add to your knowledge and understanding by sketching the live animals whenever you can.

COWS
BULLS
OXEN
STEERS

Although there are millions of cows in our country, it may well be that you have never seen one, except in pictures. It seems strange, but if you were asked to draw a lion or an elephant, you could do so with more ease than you could draw a cow.

Let's try right now to become acquainted with these gentle female animals, and then to draw them.

Upon examination you will note with surprise that, unlike most animals in the world, the cow is rather square in general appearance.

You often hear the expression "fat as a cow," but they are rarely fat and their bones always protrude sharply. The cow appears to be fat because of its great bulging trunk. But it is the wide curve of its ribs which produces this huge curving mass, rather than fat. The ribs are somewhat like the staves of a barrel, swinging wide to allow the bearing of good-sized calves.

THE HEAD

Notice the two major divisions of the head for drawing purposes. The circle encloses the area of the eyes, ears and cheeks as well as the base of the small horns. The almost square box area, shown here as a blunt oblong, contains the long mouth, the blunt nose and chin.

Try to draw these basic forms in various positions and fill in the features.

After you learn to make the diagram, make your cow's head "live" by drawing the expression.

The cow's eyes are surprisingly large and warm looking. Its lashes are long. The expression of the eye is friendly and gentle. Few people have made pets of cows. Perhaps the cow would like to change this state of affairs, because its eyes certainly are inviting and kind.

The head of a cow reflects the nature and appearance of the whole beast.

It is big and homely, and its large, limpid eyes are calm and patient.

The round, blunt nose and slow-chewing mouth are incapable of expressing anger. Most animals can sneer and make snarling expressions, but the sweet-natured cow can't look fierce even when she is most annoyed.

We use the word "bovine" to describe a calm, dull, somewhat heavy expression in some humans, and the word "bovine" pertains to the cow family.

The cow is a ruminant. Her habit of almost constantly chewing helps to give her a drowsy, quiet look.

The cow's large, blunt nose is always gleaming damply, due to her very active tongue which is constantly being thrust out of the chewing mouth to make a moist sweep over the nose and muzzle. A thick, rounded lower lip juts out under the nose, the upper lip being hidden under the nose.

The cow's ears are quite alert and at the same time floppy. They are always turning to listen for sounds which might threaten her calf or twitching to scare off flies. The ears and the fly-swatting tail are the fastest-moving parts of the cow's body.

THE LEGS

The drawings of the legs of a cow will show you the few simple divisions which we can make in order to understand the nature and action of the legs.

Very strong, yet slender and graceful, they must be able to support the great weight of the clumsy body and yet enable the animal to travel considerable distances to forage for the huge amount of food it must consume to sustain itself and perhaps an unborn calf.

Observe the points at which the legs bend. The rigid bones and the joints of the legs control the movements. The legs can bend and work only in a certain orbit. Study the movements as I have shown them here. Notice that the front legs move in quite a different manner from the hind legs, and that the shape, too, is somewhat different.

The hoof is split into two parts. This is called "cloven."

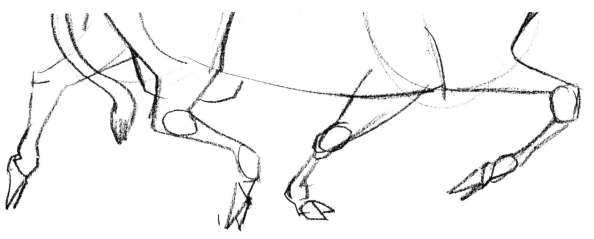

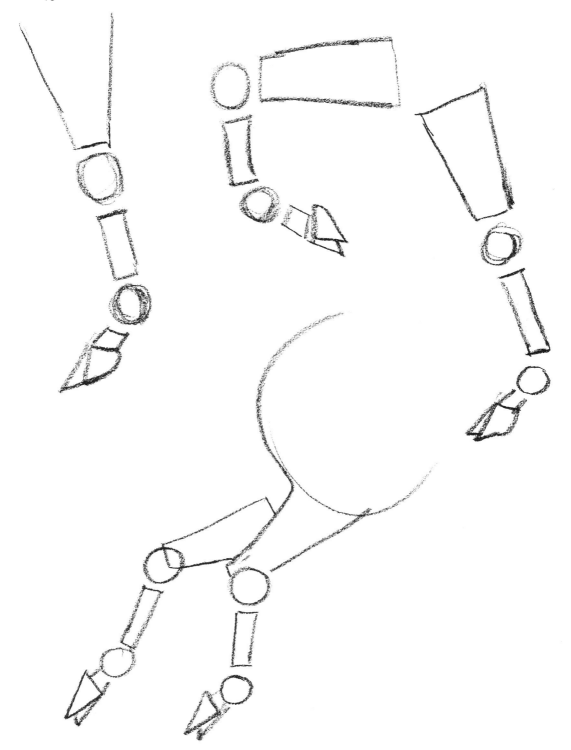

RELAXING

For their size and shape, cows can settle into surprisingly graceful and comfortable positions. They relax completely, with no taut muscles and none of the nervous alertness which seems always to be present in most animals. Cows do not seem to be much concerned with danger, and when they rest the security they feel shows in their calm poses.

BULLS

Unlike the ox, which through domestication and taming became one of the calmest and most obedient of animals, the bull is among the fiercest and most dangerous. There are stories of bulls killing lions and tigers, and we all know about the fierce bulls of the ring which are

killers by instinct and training. These traits must be borne in mind when you draw bulls.

It cannot be repeated too often to art students that far more important than the surface appearance of animals (or anything else one draws) is the spirit, the nature, the emotional character.

Learn the general aspects and proportions of the bulls shows here, and then draw their uncontrollable rage and strength and speed.

TEAM OF OXEN

Not very long ago teams of oxen were the powerful workers of most farms. They have been replaced by tractors in the United States and Britain, but are still widely used in less mechanized areas of the world.

These large beasts are strong and yet very patient and docile, and these qualities must be accented in drawing them. Their great trunks and huge heads are in contrast with their rather slender legs. But these legs, graceful and beautiful in shape, are sturdy indeed.

STEERS

Steers are male cattle. Thanks to Western movies, we all are familiar with "longhorns" and other kinds of steers that are herded for hundreds of miles across the range. As a consequence of their journeys, steers are much leaner in shape than cows and faster in movement. Here are a few examples of the different kinds of steers and a simple analysis of their general anatomy.

PIGS

I have suggested that you bear in mind the traits with which an animal is accurately associated and emphasize those traits.

More unpleasant characteristics have been attributed to the pig than to most animals, and, I'm afraid, justifiably so.

"Fat as a pig" is very descriptive. Domestic pigs are fat to begin with, and they are fattened even more for the market.

"Dirty as a pig" is also apt, because pigs like to wallow in mud and to root into the ground with their blunt noses in search of food.

"Pig-eyed" is a reference to the relatively tiny eyes in so fat and round a head.

"Pig-headed" refers to the obstinate, one-tracked way in which pigs behave.

Pigs are not as tame as most other farm animals. In fact, they can become quite dangerous when angry. Then you will notice that, in spite of the great weight on those tiny legs, they can run and turn very fast.

Draw these traits into your studies of their appearance and you will have captured the "piggishness" of the pig.

30

GOATS

Goats are only partially domesticated. Very like the cat who seems merely to tolerate us and permit us to live with him, the goat seems to have some other life in addition to the one he shares with us.

Goats have a devilish expression, an obstinacy and a sense of play which makes them unique among the quiet, patient animals of the farm.

Ancient myths and legends make the goat a symbol of wildness and revelry, and some of these traits appear in our barnyard friend of today.

There is an alertness and spryness even in the oldest males and certainly in the young ones, which makes them the clowns and at the same time the wise ones of the farm.

Goats are most at home on a steep mountainside or rocky area, where they leap from place to place with infinite agility.

Their hind legs are so powerful that they can spring many feet into the air.

Try to put some of these characteristics into your drawings.

SHEEP

Sheep are soft and timid. They bleat and "bah" and follow their leader with simple, unprotesting faith. Draw that sheeplike quality. Capture the tender, gentle expression in the eyes that gives rise to the phrase "making sheep's eyes" at someone you love.

When you draw the coat of the sheep, try to make it look fleecy, and give it the "feel" of soft, heavy masses of wool.

Except for the face and part of the nimble legs, the wool coat of the sheep tends to hide its bone structure, but with careful observation one can trace the delicate little body under the fluffy mass.

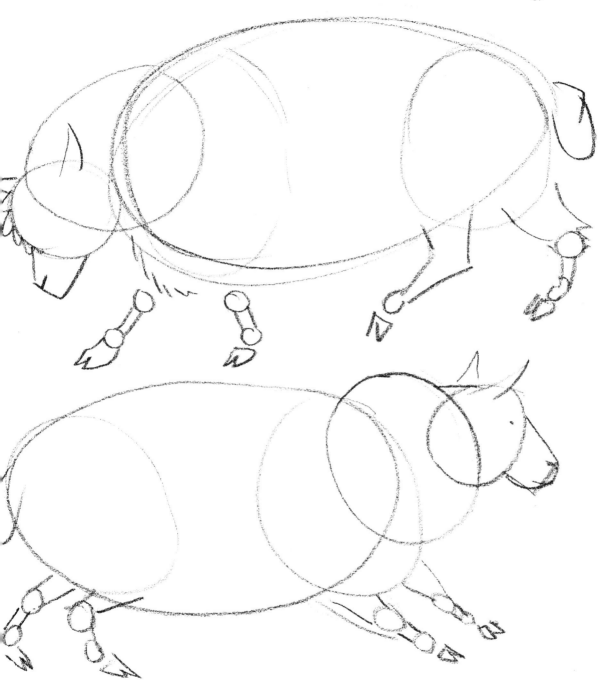

MULES

The mule is a hybrid between the horse and the donkey, and is the offspring of a male donkey and a mare.

Although similar to its parents anatomically, it has a vastly different temperament, and this should be brought out in your drawings.

"Stubborn as a mule" is the common expression, and mules can be very stubborn, indeed. But they are powerful workers and have greater endurance than most horses.

The mule's ears are not as long as a donkey's ears, but are longer than a horse's ears.

DONKEYS

Although we give the donkey a work load similar to the mule's, it is a much smaller member of the horse family and has a different nature.

Whether the expression "stupid as a donkey" is a fair one is hard to discern. The donkey seems to be thinking deeply behind its slant-eyed, withdrawn expression. If this is so, it certainly does not communicate these thoughts to us, except by an occasional harsh series of sounds of complaint called "braying."

Donkeys are obedient, patient little animals with amazing strength and endurance. They need these traits in order to put up with the long hours and enormous loads piled upon them in some parts of the world.

The general structure of the donkey is similar to that of the horse, and the method of drawing the basic form is, therefore, similar.

RABBITS

Since the rabbit is delicious food for all predatory animals, it is unfortunate that it has no weapons with which to fight. And so, as you can imagine, the wild rabbit leads a rather precarious existence. But nature has given it two compensatory gifts: a pair of the most enormous, sensitive ears in the animal kingdom; legs on which it can hop with great speed.

The rabbit is really a rodent, and its natural home is a burrow in the ground. But it has become an important farm animal and has learned to live in the hutches we build for it.

Study the postures and the means of locomotion peculiar to the rabbit. Note the difference between the hind legs and the forelegs in shape and action.

WORK HORSES

Prior to the invention of the tractor and motor truck, the horse was a commonplace part of the farmer's stock. Today, except for special horse-breeding farms, the work horse is fast disappearing from our national farm picture.

But work and plow horses are still used so much in less developed areas of the world that we must include them in our farm animal family. There is an even better reason for doing so: the work horse is among the most beautiful of animals.

Huge, powerful and patient, his form and dignity have been the subject of thousands of paintings. He will always be a beloved character to anyone who likes to draw animals.

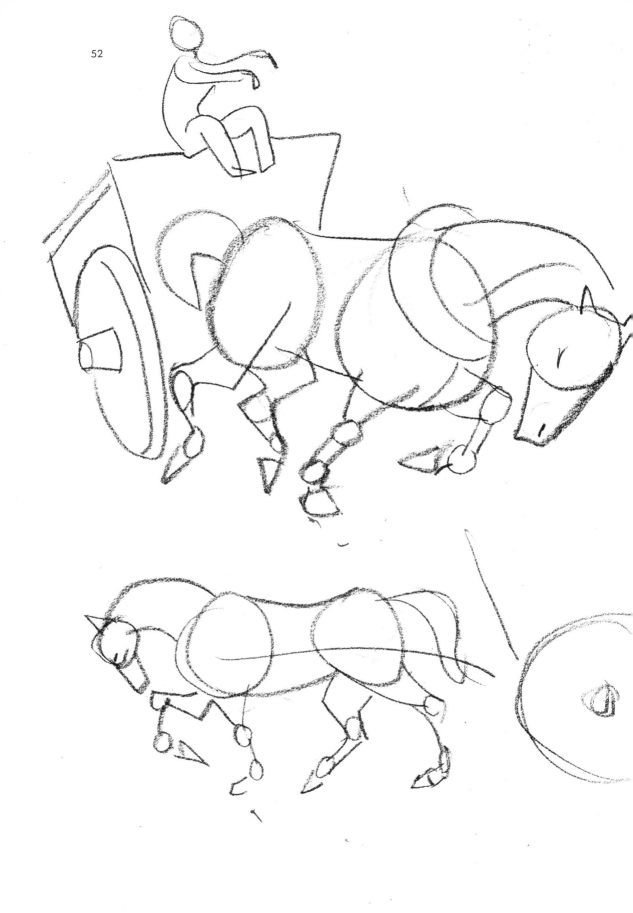

HENS ROOSTERS DUCKS TURKEYS

Domestic chickens, ducks and turkeys are not birds in character as much as they are farm animals. Flying, so characteristic of birds, is almost a forgotten art to them. Regular feeding times, familiarity with humans, and centuries of filling the jobs that humans require of them, have domesticated barnyard fowl out of that free species called "birds." Therefore, we must include them here, or our farm animal book will be incomplete.

Particularly note the walk of farm-fattened fowl, which is clumsier than that of birds that fly. They waddle or strut or hop along, each in its own individual style.

Do your best to show these special traits in your drawings. Always look for the thing to draw which will convey the characteristic that "tells the story," rather than trying for photographic likenesses.

The bodies of most birds may be reduced to a simple egg-shaped form for drawing purposes.

Make an oval; then practice placing the neck and head, wings, tail and legs in the proper place.

FIGHTING ROOSTER

Always remember that drawing is vastly different from photography.
The camera captures everything that is exposed to its lens in a split
second. But you must search for the main thing to be said in your
drawings. You not only see, you think while you draw. As I did in
this drawing of a fighting rooster, you must accent what is important
and leave out the rest.

62.